T0126498

Creating Unity

Creating Unity

The Guide to Leading a Marriage Support Group

Angela AND Chris Yousey

NEW YORK

LONDON • NASHVILLE • MELBOURNE • VANCOUVER

Creating Unity
The Guide to Leading a Marriage Support Group

© 2020 Angela and Chris Yousey

Published in New York, New York, by Morgan James Publishing in partnership with Difference Press. Morgan James is a trademark of Morgan James, LLC.
www.MorganJamesPublishing.com

ISBN 9781642797206 paperback
ISBN 9781642797213 eBook
ISBN 9781642797459 audiobook
Library of Congress Control Number: 2019945477

Cover Design by:
Chris Treccani
www.3dogcreative.net

Interior Design by:
Christopher Kirk
www.GFSstudio.com

Scripture quotations marked AMP taken from the Amplified® Bible (AMP), Copyright © 2015 by The Lockman Foundation. Used by permission. www.Lockman.org

Scripture quotations marked MSG are taken from THE MESSAGE, copyright © 1993, 2002, 2018 by Eugene H. Peterson. Used by permission of NavPress. All rights reserved. Represented by Tyndale House Publishers, Inc.

Scripture quotations marked NASB taken from the New American Standard Bible® (NASB), Copyright © 1960, 1962, 1963, 1968, 1971, 1972, 1973, 1975, 1977, 1995 by The Lockman Foundation. Used by permission. www.Lockman.org

Scripture marked NIV taken from the Holy Bible, NEW INTERNATIONAL VERSION®, NIV® Copyright © 1973, 1978, 1984, 2011 by Biblica, Inc.® Used by permission. All rights reserved worldwide.

Morgan James is a proud partner of Habitat for Humanity Peninsula and Greater Williamsburg. Partners in building since 2006.

Get involved today! Visit
MorganJamesPublishing.com/giving-back

Table of Contents

Chapter 1:	You Can Lead A Marriage Group	1
Chapter 2:	Walking Through the Process	5
Chapter 3:	The Difference You Will Make	11
Chapter 4:	A Wife's Greatest Need	15
Chapter 5:	A Man's Greatest Need	21
Chapter 6:	Communication or Connection	27
Chapter 7:	Resolving Conflict Do's and Don'ts	35
Chapter 8:	Protecting Love	43
Chapter 9:	Money, Why Budget?	49
Chapter 10:	Sex	55
Chapter 11:	Obstacles Families May Face	61
Chapter 12:	Get Ready to Start a Movement	67

Acknowledgments 69
Thank You. 71
About the Authors. 73

Chapter 1:

You Can Lead a Marriage Group

It is sad to say, but there is a fifty-fifty chance of being successful in marriage. It is one of the most important decisions that one can make, yet there is very little preparation for after the big day. On average, couples devote about ten hours every week for more than a year preparing for the wedding, which lasts less than an hour. They assume that the rest of their lives will magically last with no preparation. Studies say that nearly seventy percent of all churches do not` have a marriage ministry. Studies also show that even most mega-churches with up to ten children and youth pastors don't have a full-time marriage pastor. Most churches focus on family ministries, which usually concentrate on making sure that kids are having fun while parents watch. I believe that most pastors don't realize how to minister to marriages and are often unaware of how to be successfully married themselves.

Many would think that to conduct a marriage ministry, one would be required to be a pastor or a licensed therapist. The truth is, all it takes is someone who has the love of God and a good marriage (not a perfect one). There is no such thing as a perfect marriage. This has been an excuse for many pastors to shy away from forming a marriage ministry. They feel that they would not have a right to have such a ministry when they themselves have a rocky relationship. The other reality is that pastors can't do it all.

If you are consistently working on your own marriage trying to become more Christ-like, then it will also make you a good candidate for a marriage ministry. Couples are looking for those to whom they can look to for guidance. I have found that couples will connect more with you when they feel they can relate. You don't have to be perfect in your relationship, and you never will. If you are willing to be transparent about your own marital struggles and victories, those you lead will follow.

As you sow into the lives of others' marriages, you will be sowing into yours as well. This book will remind you of its principles and will help you stay accountable. One study revealed that eighty percent of couples who do premarital counseling stay together. The impact you will have on marriages will be astounding. The reward of seeing couples flourish and families kept together is the greatest blessing.

Inside the pages of this book, we will lay out the principles of marriage counseling in an easy-to-read format. Whether you want to lead a small group or provide one-on-one biblical guidance on marriage, the tools are here so that you will be able to lead your group with confidence.

What we share is exactly what we have taught for many years. In the chapters ahead, you will know how to put into words ways to bring unity to marriage. Wives will understand how to encourage their husbands to become the best man for her. Husbands will know what they can do to help their wives blossom into the lover of his dreams. You will be able to explain effective communication skills and how to apply them. Disagreements happen in every relationship. Disagreement causes us to grow closer or farther apart. You will be able to instruct how to work through disagreements in a way that will draw couples close. Finances are the number one cause of divorce. You will be able to explain how finances can be managed in a way that will ensure financial freedom. Sex is supposed to be fun for both the husband and wife. You will be able to discuss how to be satisfied in the bedroom. Upon completion of this book, you will know that you are ready to lead your group into a happy marriage.

Chapter 2:

Walking Through the Process

At the age of twenty-one, I married my college sweetheart. Although I was young and inexperienced, I was willing to allow him to have my full heart. In my mind, I had the perfect marriage that was shielded from any possibility of divorce. We were financially stable. We seemed to have the same goals and dreams. I was happy, and I assumed he was too. In the fourth year of our marriage, my world shook when I discovered that my husband was having an affair. It devastated me, but in my heart, I felt that it was part of the process to fulfill my calling.

The pain I felt that night when I discovered his infidelity was deep. I remember walking into my house feeling like the blood had been drained from my body. I fell into my bed gripping the pillow with tears streaming in a continuous flow. I curled up in a fetal position, trying to neutralize the pain to my soul. It was as if someone reached inside and tore my guts out. I had been a good wife and didn't understand why he would want to do this to our family. We had a three-year-old son who would now be without his father.

I never got angry with God because I believed that it was the path to my destiny. I spent much time in prayer and searched the word of God for anything that resonated hope. I never once doubted that I would come out of this storm stronger and more prepared for the calling of restoring marriages. I would pray and tell God how bad it hurt but that I trusted Him to do whatever He needed to prepare me for His purpose.

I hoped that my husband would have a change of heart and return home, but he never did. The day that the court granted the divorce, I stood on the steps of the courthouse as the tears streamed from my face. I cried out to God, "If this is what it will take to be able to understand how to help hurting marriages, then I will accept."

Several months after the divorce, I moved to Columbus, Ohio to start my new career as a registered nurse. I was brave at only twenty-four years old with a three-year-old son. I didn't know anyone and moving to a large city was frightening.

One night, a year after I moved to Columbus, I picked my son up from the sitter and decided to go to church for a special service. My son sometimes had a hard time sitting still, so I made a deal with him. I told him that if he was good during church, I would take him to a restaurant called Cracker Barrel. The church seated over 5,000 people, and there was an overflow that was filling up by the time I arrived. I walked up to an usher, and while nodding my head "no" in doubt, I asked if there was a seat anywhere for us. At the moment, the usher noticed a man leaving from the balcony area. He stated that we could have his seat if I held my son. I gladly accepted. However, as I worked my way through the seats, I realized that there was a little boy seated there. The boy's father insisted that I take the seat as long as I was okay with our two sons to sit on the floor. I thanked the kind man and sat down.

Immediately the little boy whispered to my son, "Hi, my name is Mike, and we have to be good because my daddy said that he would take me to Crackle Barrel if I am good." I was in total shock to hear the same deal offered to the little white boy. After church, the kind man named Chris and his son insisted that since they were good, we should go to the restaurant together. There he shared of his past about his ex-wife: how she had an affair, how she was addicted to drugs, and how he was awarded sole custody of their three-year-old son. Our stories were identical. There was no doubt in my mind that this was a connection made by God. The following year, we married, and in that same year, we gave birth to our first son together. My family was growing and fast. My husband's ex-wife also had another son, whom she was unfit to raise. She called me to ask if we would raise him as well. He was only three years old. We had gone from one son to four sons in one year. A few years later, we gave birth to two more sons for a total of six.

I often expressed my frustration to my husband. He was always a listening ear even when I directed my frustrations toward the kids. I knew that I shouldn't feel this way and wanted things to feel differently. I stayed close to my husband because he had proven that I could trust and depend on him. We developed the habit of praying together as a foundation of our marriage. We would ask God for His wisdom on how to merge our two families together and God answered.

Two of the keys to our success are unity and love. Being an interracial couple, it doesn't matter of our outward differences. We have always protected each other. Whenever our insecurities and past hurts would arise, we would reassure each other that we were on the same team. Our love brought healing to us, and our trust grew stronger. We fostered a home of love and unity and desired a peaceful home for our children. Our sons grew to be friends, and we never allowed race to be an issue.

Other couples in our community and church noticed us, and some would ask if we would counsel them. The couples would come to our home to learn of our secrets to a successful marriage and a peaceful home. The groups grew so large that some would sit on the floor. I remember one class in our home was so large that my husband and I stood in the corner of the room to teach because there was no place to sit. With high divorce rates, more people have not seen a successful marriage to mimic. Every week, there would be a couple in our home for counseling. Many times, they would come in crying and angry and would leave free and holding hands. The reward of witnessing couples falling in love again and being a part of it is worth our sacrifice. Couples came from churches we had never heard of. Couples would tell their friends, and then they would come too. We felt that in order to help people on a greater scale, we needed to start a church. It was not something we had ever done; however, we knew how to pray for God's wisdom.

One night, I got up at 3 a.m. to study and pray. I heard in my spirit to get on Craigslist to look for church chairs and to look outside of the city. I opened my laptop and typed in, "Craigslist Ohio." To my amazement, all of the cities popped up! I thought, I don't have time to look through every city listed. I said in my heart, "Now what, God?" I felt that He was saying to click on Dayton, so I did. The first posting that popped up was 150 church chairs a church wanted to donate to another church. They had decided to upgrade their existing church furniture. We were the first to respond to the post, as they had just posted it a few hours prior. We knew that that was a clear sign we were to start a church to be able to help people on a larger scale. We then had 150 chairs but nowhere to put them.

About two months later, Regina, a faithful follower, sent me a Craigslist posting about a church rental. I contacted them the very next morning. They told me there were many interested people and they would be meeting in about two weeks to decide who they would select to rent the space. We had such a peace about it. We knew that God had blessed us to help families. We knew that all we needed to do was to be obedient. A few days later, we received a call stating that we were hands-down offered the building. We had no idea that twenty-five years ago one or two couples sitting in our living room would lead to this. We would simply share how we lived, not even considering that it was counseling. Now we not only co-pastor at Spirit of Love Ministries in Columbus, Ohio, but we are also assisting other churches in developing marriage ministry leaders.

Chapter 3:

The Difference You Will Make

You can learn how to become that resource of change couples are begging for. No one gets married with the idea of getting divorced. We speak to couples often who want to know more to keep their marriage intact. They are not expecting you to know all the answers to all things, but what you do know, they will take. Learning what's here will equip you with the confidence to potentially change a generation and those to come.

We met with a couple last evening. When we first started working with them, they constantly spoke of how they had been hurt by one another. The husband had an affair in the past, and she was angry about it for years after. Their marriage wasn't moving forward because they were stuck in the past. We listened to their concerns and then inquired when the affair happened. It happened over fifteen years ago. We asked if there was another affair after that one, which they both denied. We asked, "Do you see what is happening here?" They were giving so much energy to the place of hurt instead of the place of healing. They were holding on to the past as a reminder of where they never wanted to return to. In reality, they had never left that place. They never allowed those old wounds to heal. They together kept picking away at the scabs. We asked them if they were ready for change. They agreed that they were, but didn't know how. The first step to healing is forgiveness, and they were willing to do whatever it took to move on.

There have been times where someone says no, that they can't forgive, or they aren't ready to do so. This is the first step to recovery. In this case, the wife would use the guilt of offense as leverage. The wife would remind the husband of what he did in hopes that he would pour out love as restitution. He did so from a place of duty rather than a place of purity of heart. This led to dissatisfaction for both of them. This quote best describes unforgiveness: "Holding onto resentment is like drinking poison and expecting the other person to die." Letting go of old hurts puts you in a vulnerable place because it opens your heart up to be possibly hurt again. We led them in a prayer of forgiveness, and it was beautiful to witness. They wept and embraced as the healing process began. This is only the beginning of a long road to recovery. Just saying words of forgiveness isn't the end but rather the beginning. The temptation will be there to return to the place of hurt, to pick at the scab again. We remind them that picking at the scab is like being in a pit you can't get out of. The more you dig in a pit, the deeper it gets. Reminding them to resist going back into the pit is also key. Forgiveness is a skill that one must practice often in order to keep his or her relationship healthy. Let go of the small offenses that turn you back toward the pit.

When we first got married, somehow we understood this principle. We understood that we were not each other's enemy. We view ourselves as one and the same. If one of us hurts, then we both hurt. If I hurt my husband, then I hurt myself. Let me explain. There is such peace and power when we are in unity. It is an energy that you feel, and others notice. My husband is a very kind and giving person. He will give his time and money. I, on the other hand, am the budget patrol. He once wanted to help a family in need at Christmas, so he purchased their entire Christmas for them. We had all six of our sons at home who we had to buy for as well. I yelled at him and stormed off to work. I knew that I had hurt him, and our unity had been severed. I wasn't entirely wrong in what I thought and felt; however, the way that I handled it was. There is a way to effectively communicate my frustrations in a way that does not disrupt unity. We are quick to forgive because unforgiveness tears us apart while forgiveness draws us closer together. I speak more to this in Chapter 6.

There is nothing more rewarding than seeing a couple walk into our home heavy and seeing them leave with a smile, holding hands. Seeing them sit on opposite ends of our sofa, hugging. There is nothing like having children hug you for helping bring their daddy and mommy back together. The bible says in Matthew 5:9 (MSG), "You're blessed when you can show people how to cooperate instead of compete or fight. That's when you discover who you really are and your place in God's family."

Chapter 4:

A Wife's Greatest Need

"And now these three remain: faith, hope and love.
But the greatest of these is love."
– 1 Corinthians 13:13 (NIV)

The way you express love is by doing. Growing up, I had never seen a marriage of two people who were truly in love. I thought I did until I experienced it. In my mind, I thought real love is when a husband and wife are faithful to one another. Go on trips together, go to dinner, stay faithful, and make love regularly. This all sounds great, but there is so much more!

When I met Chris, I felt that he was a kind and caring man. When we were together, I always enjoyed it, but subconsciously,

I was afraid to allow myself to be vulnerable. I was an independent registered nurse, single parent divorcee with a lot of hurts. In my heart, I wanted to show him all the love and affection he deserved, but I didn't know how. I remember him saying that he wished I could express my heart to him. He seemed to want to know everything about me. He was able to share how much he loved me, how much he missed me throughout the day. He needed to touch me and hold me at night. To be honest, I felt it was a bit annoying. I would tell him I didn't need that kind of attention.

Chris knew there had to be more to marriage than what he was getting. He studied the scripture. One of his favorite scriptures was, Ephesians 5:25, "Husbands, love your wives [seek the highest good for her and surround her with a caring, unselfish love], just as Christ also loved the church and gave Himself up for her, so that He might sanctify the church, having cleansed her by the washing of water with the word [of God]."

He began to shower me with love. He truly believed that the wife he desired and the one I wanted to become was buried within. He treated me with such care that I knew he valued me as precious. He thought of me in ways I wouldn't imagine. On Fridays, Chris would take my car and fill the gas tank so I wouldn't have to get out in the cold. One winter, as I left for work, I noticed a car just like mine parked beside the exit door.

He had driven to my job to clear the snow off my car, heat it up, and pick me up at the door. This was a perfect example of Eph 5:25 – of "surround her with a caring, unselfish love."

It wasn't until I lost my job when I realized that I really needed him. I was depressed and hurt and felt that my identity had been stripped from me. Chris fought for me in prayer. He prayed over me and for me. He constantly reminded me of my worth. He spoke of my gifts and talents when everything in me said I was unworthy and unfit. Just as Christ declared his word over his people (church) to transform us, so did my husband for me. The more he affirmed me, the more his words cleansed me of my past. Before long, I believed I was who he said I was. I cannot tell you that the process of love is for the faint at heart, but I can tell you it works if you don't quit. 1 Corinthians 13:7 New Living Translation (NLT) says, "Love never gives up, never loses faith, is always hopeful, and endures through every circumstance." Now, we are both thoughtful of each one another. I now enjoy surprising him with his favorite meal from the Olive Garden. I enjoy supporting him when he speaks at a church, even if it means only holding his water.

Here are some love suggestions you could share with couples:

- Hug and kiss her every day before leaving for work.
- Hold her hand while driving
- Call, not text, just to say, "I love you."

- Make her breakfast in bed
- Don't criticize her, but rather, praise her.

My husband was not okay with doing life together yet separate. He wanted more for us and knew our strength was greater together as one. It was not easy for him to give his time in praying for me, in confessing the word over me. He simply would not move on unless I was moving with him. He truly believed we were members of each other (one body). If I am hurting in my body, he is hurting. Ephesians 5:28 says, "Even so husbands should *and* are morally obligated to love their own wives as [being in a sense] their own bodies. He who loves his own wife loves himself. For no one ever hated his own body, but [instead] he nourishes *and* protects and cherishes it, just as Christ does the church," because we are members (parts) of His body.

Sometimes my restless legs keep me up at night. If he senses they are bothering me, he sits up in bed and rubs them until I am able to find relief. He would tell me it's because he loved me.

It took me several years to realize this unconditional love is exactly what I needed in order to become who God and my husband needed for me to be. It was then I was able to love and let love. Today, I am not afraid to be transparent in my love and affection to him. I love being with him. There is nothing more beautiful than when he shares his deepest thoughts and fantasies with me and mine with him. It creates such a beautiful, intimate connection I never dreamed possible.

When speaking to couples, we make it clear that it won't change overnight. We encourage them to be patient but diligent. You will reap a harvest from the seeds of life that you plant. On the other hand, you can speak words of death and reap a harvest from that. Proverbs 18:20-22 says, "A man's belly shall be satisfied with the fruit of his mouth; and with the increase of his lips shall he be filled. Death and life are in the power of the tongue: and they that love it shall eat the fruit thereof."

I know that a husband and wife can create whatever they want in a marriage. We have seen and counseled many couples that do not speak life into each other. Couples have the ability to speak life or death into their spouse. We discourage speaking words like lazy, unromantic, boring, mean, etc. Words are seeds that will return to you. A powerful way to speak life is by prayer. During every session, we remind the couples to pray together daily and to speak life over one another and their families.

Chapter 5:

A Man's Greatest Need

E arly on in our marriage, I used to go crazy trying to think of ways to get Chris to do and see things my way. I would insult him by voicing my frustrations with him in front of our children. It was probably the most damaging action on my part. I discovered that he would instantly disconnect with me. It would sometimes take days before I would sense emotion from him. We would go through the motions as if all was well, but it would be clear that there was a wall up.

I love the interpretation of Ephesians 5:33 Amplified Bible (AMP), "...the wife [must see to it] that she respects *and* delights in her husband [that she notices him and prefers him and treats him with loving concern, treasuring him, honoring him, and holding him dear]." There were times that it was hard to show respect for him, especially when I felt I was right. I thought if I would sternly voice my anger, then he would change. Tearing him down only lead to him feeling rejected, and he, in turn, rejected me. Men love to feel as if they are the king in your life, so I honored him more and corrected or criticized him less. Remember to remind those you counsel that it takes dedication and maturity, but remember to remind those you counsel that it takes dedication and maturity. If the wives apply these qualities, they will begin to see change happen in their man.

I remember receiving two dozen long stem roses delivered to my work. All my co-workers thought it was the most beautiful thing he could do. I, instead, was angry because he wasted all that money on roses that would be dead in a few short days. My reaction crushed him. I had missed an opportunity to honor him. He later told me that all he wanted to feel was my satisfaction with him.

We have been married for twenty-seven years, and to this day, he opens my car door for me. The first time that my mother witnessed this, I told her that I am not handicapped and that I can open my own door. She corrected me by saying that most women would be delighted to have a man like mine. I felt deeply remorseful and began thanking him every time. I noticed that it makes him feel good when I brag about him to my friends and family. As you counsel, encourage women to find something he does that they respect and build on it. It may be small at first. Maybe it's as simple as recognizing him for putting his dirty clothes in the clothes basket instead of on the floor. Honor and respect him for the small things, and soon he will change in other areas to gain more of your respect.

Recently my husband and I worked with a couple that was strange because during our session with them the husband had nothing to say. Finally, by the third session, he stated that he had learned to keep his mouth shut because he didn't want to be treated like a child. We asked exactly what that meant. He felt that his opinion didn't matter. His wife would say things like "You don't make sense," and "My way is better." He stood before us like a wounded dog. God created man to have a natural desire to be respected, and he will find someone that will respect him if his wife doesn't.

Years ago, we worked with a couple in our church. Whenever the husband would speak, the wife would cross her arms and roll her eyes. He got frustrated and voiced that he hated it when she would do that and that he felt disrespected. She asked how she could be disrespectful when she didn't say a word. Words don't always reveal disrespect. Actions can also reveal it.

We taught these principles in our marriage classes. We would give them an assignment to love and honor each other the following week. When they returned to class, we had each couple share how the week went. Their responses were always moving. What they would share were simple things such as, my wife supported me when disciplining their kids and the husband appreciated it. Another husband said that his wife said thanks for taking the trash to the curb. Someone else stated that when he returned from work, his wife got off the phone with her best friend and that made him feel special. Always make sure your clients know to look for ways to show respect toward each other.

Here are some ways you can suggest couples show respect:

- **Don't withhold intimacies.** He will feel rejected.
- **Spend time with him.** Just be together.
- **Don't bad mouth him to extended family.** This will cause him to feel disrespected by others in the family.
- **Show support on parenting,** especially in front of the children.
- **Praise him in front of family and friends.** It will make him feel good in front of those that mean the most to him.
- **Become his cheerleader.** Encouragement instead of criticizing will cause him to feel respected.
- **Let him know you need him.** Even if you really can do it yourself, such as having him change the windshield wipers on your car or unclogging the drain.

- **Say you are sorry.** It will let him know that you care about his feelings.
- **Acknowledge him when he comes home.** This reminds him that he is important to you.
- **Tell him you miss him when apart.** He will know that he is on your mind.
- **Tell him he's handsome.** It will let him know that you have eyes only for him.
- **Touch him.** Touch is a language. It will say many things such as peace, desire, and love.

Chapter 6:

Communication or Connection

Communication is so much more than words. Usually, when we speak to couples about communication, we have found that it's not actually talking that's the issue but rather connection. There are times that my husband and I can sit silently enjoying being together and feeling most understood. Likewise, have you ever met with a friend and left feeling like you never emotionally connected or our conversation seemed to have never started? I remember a time while shopping during the holidays I stood in line with a lady. She and I talked about how much of a great deal we were getting on the same items we were purchasing. We talked about the same stores we planned to shop at. We shared coupons and even online options. There was such a connection there that before we went our separate ways we hugged. We never heard each other's names, but we shared an emotional moment that fostered communication.

I don't want to give the impression that communication isn't important because it is vital in any relationship. When I pondered what connected me to the lady in the checkout line, I noticed that it was our passion for the same things and the ability to discuss them. Many couples that struggle in the area of communication do so because they have not found commonality.

When we first started our business, my husband spoke nonstop about it. I felt that the business was a great source of stress, so avoiding that conversation was fine with me. He became frustrated because he wanted to share his progress with me. That frustration led to feelings of disrespect and unappreciation for his hard work. I saw how he acted when he shared with other business people, how much passion and life he spoke with. I asked questions and listened to him. It wasn't easy to start, but in order to improve connection, you have to find the right adapters. The right adapter for this situation was to be willing to discuss what is important to one another.

One of the most magical turning points in our marriage was when we discovered that one of us could be right or wrong. There is nothing more frustrating than when one spouse feels as if his or her opinion isn't valued. We sat with a couple, and every time we asked a question, the husband would answer for the wife. Finally, we asked for him to let his wife speak for herself. To our surprise, she had a lot to say and made some very valid points. Spouses should always be willing to listen to each other, no matter how right they feel they are. My husband is slow to decide on big moves. I, on the other hand, am not. Chris also takes longer to get to his points than I do. I used to go nuts in my head waiting for him to prove his point. I have learned that when I slow down to hear him, we almost always make the better decision, and if we don't, we are both to blame.

One of the main reasons why people don't share what's really in their hearts is because it places them in a very vulnerable place. When we first married, the way my husband could easily share his deepest feelings amazed me. Even on our very first date, he told me of how he had been hurt in his prior relationship and how his heart was crushed. I, too, had been hurt but was afraid to share. I wondered why I was afraid. I knew that it was an issue for me but didn't know how to fix the problem. After several years of evaluating myself, I realized that I was afraid of rejection. Before my husband, I had been able to share my deepest thoughts with a man who, in the end, hurt me. I subconsciously was going to protect my heart from ever experiencing such pain again. My husband had never hurt me, yet I was not willing to fully allow him to love me emotionally.

One evening we sat on the couch and my husband shared how much he loved me and how he had missed me so much throughout the day. He stated that he just wanted to hold me. I had never said anything like that to him. I shared how I wished I could be that open about my emotions. His reply was perfect, "I will never reject or hurt you, will you try to trust me?" It is wonderful to experience unity in our relationship. Everything isn't perfect, but here are a few principles that we have found to work that you can introduce to your clients.

Mirroring is a communication strategy that we like to use. We teach couples this technique when couples say that they don't feel as if their mate is hearing them. In this exercise, the spouse would express their feelings; once they have completed their thought, the other spouse would then repeat what they feel they heard. Instruct the spouse listening to start by saying, "What I think I heard was…" or "Are you saying…?" Mirroring can help a spouse test whether he or she is hearing his or her spouse properly. Once the spouse talking makes a point, instruct the spouse listening to repeat it to him or her by saying something like, "So, what I hear you saying is…" or "Are you saying…?" At the end of the exercise, it is important to allow each spouse to affirm or correct what he or she said.

Marriage is supposed to be fun! No one would ever get married if they believed that in two years the laughter, romance, and communication would stop. Remind couples to keep it current and remain emotionally connected. What they did to get him or her to say "I do" is what needs to continue. When we were dating, we went camping, bowling, to the movies, and traveled. We would have date nights at home and away. My husband would order take out, and we would sit and talk. We would play board games and laugh at each other's jokes. We have kept all of these practices current. In other words, don't let your friendship die. He is my best friend, and we love to be together.

Couples that pray together stay together. Praying together is one of the most powerful things couples could do. Encourage your clients to pray together so that they will hear what is near and dear to their mate's heart. No one ever wastes time praying for things that don't matter much. When praying, most people are asking about what is most important. There are times when we pray that I am surprised by what comes from my husband's mouth. Daily, he covers me in prayer and asks God to help him to be the husband that I need, to give me wisdom to make good decisions on my job, to come and go safely. I pray that he has great favor when negotiating business deals, for wisdom, and strength. If there is anything that concerns us, we will pray. When we invite God to be a part of our daily lives, we don't need to figure life out alone. Connecting to God together binds us together with one heart in God. Beautiful, intimate times are shared when we open our hearts to God together. This connection fosters unity, love, and protection. Because I know my husband will call upon the wisdom of God to help us, I am quick to share my heart with him.

Divorce rates between married Christians that attend church regularly is about fifty percent. With couples that pray together daily, the divorce rate drops to one out of 1,153, according to one Gallup Poll. Matthew 18:19-20 (NLT) says, "I also tell you this: If two of you agree here on earth concerning anything you ask, my Father in heaven will do it for you. For where two or three gather together as my followers, I am there among them." God is saying that when you invite Him into your affairs, He will be there, and the best part is He will give you what you need. We have seen this happen many times. Often before we discuss an important matter, we first invite the wisdom of God. He knows us best, and he also knows what's best for us.

Before we started our church, we had to first find a building. We never dreamed that it would be so painfully difficult. Finally, we found a small place that we thought would work for a little while. The location was perfect, and the rent was affordable. Everything about it appeared to be for us until we prayed. A few days after we asked for Gods wisdom, we both felt uneasy in our hearts. We had already signed the lease, had it notarized, and enclosed the cashier's check for the first three months. We knew that we weren't to give it to the landlord. We prayed about it several times because we didn't want to make a big financial mistake that would pull on our marriage. We teach couples to always follow after peace. That means, in your heart, if you don't feel good about something, then wait. We prayed about it for a couple of months. We then learned of another building that was in a better location than the first, and it was 10,000 square feet larger than the first and less expensive. Prayer not only helps with communication, but it also helps keep us connected and moving in the right direction that God has for us. Proverbs 12:18 (NLT)

Some people make cutting remarks, but the words of the wise bring healing. Gods words are always wise so encourage couples to pray and to speak God's words over their marriage. Ephesians 4:29 (NLT) Don't use foul or abusive language. Let everything you say be good and helpful so that your words will be an encouragement to those who hear them. Encourage couples to address one another as if they are an invited guest. When you invite a special guest, you are trying to develop a connection, and you use words to encourage. Couples should work at exercising this principle, as it will cause their communication to flourish.

Chapter 7:

Resolving Conflict Do's and Don'ts

Early on in our marriage if I was angry about something while in public, I used to correct Chris. I have always been a strong personality that some would call "bossy." I have been blessed with common sense, and when those around me make poor choices, I tend to get frustrated. One thing that I have discovered is no matter how strongly you feel you are right, it is possible to be wrong. I at least should listen to his opinion. Every couple has disagreements from time to time, which should help to grow deeper in our relationship. If conflict is handled in a healthy way, most conflicts can be resolved, and the couple should be able to make peace. Here are some of the Do's and Don'ts on fighting.

Never Fight in Public

Fighting should always be done in private. You should be free to express your feelings and thoughts without being concerned with onlookers. It is very dishonoring to your mate. When I would snap at my husband in public, he would instantly get quiet. He has never tolerated arguing in public. Fighting is a private encounter that should foster growth. Public display of anger toward your spouse is not only disrespectful, but it may also cause others to lose respect as well.

Take a Time Out

There have been times during an argument when I was in a rush to the finish line. He was going to hear me out no matter what. My voice would escalate, and my body language would intensify. Not long after, my husband would purse his lips. If he felt that the argument was going in a direction that would cause more damage than good, he would say, "We can't talk about this now." We would take some time to cool down until we were ready to effectively talk.

Describe How You Feel

In order to keep the guards down when arguing, avoid starting the conversation with "You." Try starting the conversation with "I feel" instead. "I feel angry" rather than "You make me angry." When you start the argument with "Why did you…," "You always…," or "How could you…," you place the blame for the argument on them. If you start out by saying "I feel angry because…," you are setting up for open and productive dialogue.

Always Show Respect

Remember, you are on the same team. The focus of every disagreement should be to resolve it so that you grow deeper together.

Be Patient

There is nothing more overwhelming than waiting to get something off your chest. The worst thing that you can do to diminish your chances of resolving conflict is to force a conversation. If your mate says that they need more time to process things, then respect them enough to allow the space. If you are the one asking for the space, then be sure to revisit the conversation in a timely manner. If left unresolved, it will lead to greater frustrations.

Respect Each Other's Opinions

Once again, you are not always right. I remind myself of why I married my husband in the first place. He is kind, loving, and smart. He sees things from a different lens than me. I have learned that if I allow him to express himself and express myself to him, we are able to hear the value in both opinions. This has been a major key for us. Sometimes I feel like I need duct tape and need to sit on my hands, but I have experienced the outcome, and it's worth it.

Walk In Their Shoes

This principle applies to any communication. Things always look different from the other side. When we are discussing our differences, I evaluate myself by asking, "How would I feel if I were in his shoes?" "Would I feel the same if the tables were turned?" Often, I can see the error in my ways, and what was once a conflict for us worked itself out.

Don't Laugh at Your Spouse

Talk about pouring gas on the fire! Laughing at your spouse's opinion during a disagreement says many things. It makes them feel like their thoughts are farfetched, silly, and unreceived. It will cause them to not trust and to resent their mate. Laughing at them also makes them feel as if you don't find them to be intelligent.

Don't Yell

People raise their voices because they are emotionally frustrated or feel as if they are not heard. If both partners are yelling, then no one is being heard. The focus shifts from the issue at hand to the yelling match and nothing is resolved.

> *"Hot tempers start fights; a calm, cool spirit*
> *keeps the peace."*
> – Proverbs 15:18 (MSG)

Don't Fight Over What Has Already Been Resolved

We work with couples that have been stuck on a certain disagreement. They have forgiven each other time and time again, yet it keeps coming up. Agree to let it go and move on. If not, it will cause your relationship to stagnate. Any healthy relationship should be growing.

They Are Not Mind Readers

Don't assume that your spouse can read your mind just because you are so angry about the issue. They may be totally unaware of what is happening. You owe it to them and yourself to clearly explain your thoughts.

Select a Third Party Wisely

Try to resolve your conflicts between you two. If you feel the need to seek help from a third party, then do so wisely. The third party should be someone that you both agree upon and should be someone unbiased.

Are your kids watching?

The way they will learn to communicate is mainly through you. You have the power and ability to teach your children how to resolve conflict by your example. What an opportunity!

Don't Go to Bed Angry

If possible, try to resolve any conflicts before going to bed. Going to bed angry makes a long, unpleasant night. If you can't seem to reach a resolution, then try to agree to stay at peace with each other throughout the night.

> *"'In your anger, do not sin;' do not let the sun go down while you are still angry."*
> – Ephesians 4:26 (New International Version)

Forgive

Don't hold on to unforgiveness. If you are in the wrong, learn to say sorry. It shows humility and a desire to resolve conflict. Be clear about what it is that you are sorry about. For example, "I am sorry that I…"

*"Don't force your spouse to move to accept your forgiveness.
Let them do so on their time."*
– Colossians 3:13 (MSG)

So, chosen by God for this new life of love, dress in the wardrobe God picked out for you: compassion, kindness, humility, quiet strength, discipline. Be even-tempered, content with second place, quick to forgive an offense. Forgive as quickly and completely as the Master forgave you. And regardless of what else you put on, wear love. It's your basic, all-purpose garment. Never be without it.

Pray

Ask God for help. We have learned that when we pray prior to a conflict, it changes our heart toward the direction of what God would want for us, for us to be in unity and love.

"Don't fret or worry. Instead of worrying, pray. Let petitions and praises shape your worries into prayers, letting God know your concerns. Before you know it, a sense of God's wholeness, everything coming together for good, will come and settle you down. It's wonderful what happens when Christ displaces worry at the center of your life."
– Philippians 4:6-7 (MSG)

Chapter 8:

Protecting Love

Not long ago, a couple called us to their home to help them resolve a conflict. The wife was upset that her husband had lent money to a friend without consulting with her first. The husband was upset with the wife because she spent too much time with her extended family. After they both got it all off their chests, I then asked them both, "What is the common denominator to all of your problems?" They looked at each other and stated family and friends. I said, "Bingo!" Your priority is to protect your marriage and home. You must readjust anything that interrupts the flow of unity. I advised them to narrow down the friend list and to limit the number of days that one spends with extended family. I call it simplifying life. Two weeks after our meeting, they reported that it had turned their relationship around one hundred percent.

We raised six sons, and all of them played sports; I was the team mom for three of the boys' teams in one season. There was so much laundry that we had two washers and two dryers. We used six gallons of milk weekly and six jars of spaghetti sauce when making spaghetti. In all of this, we have always protected our time together. We can feel it when we are growing disconnected. Our children knew the rule that if mom and dad's door is closed, then do NOT disturb them. There are some things that one must take care of that may be taxing, such as the kids' sport schedules, but there is no other relationship more important than the one with your spouse. All others must take a back seat. Sunday was the day that we would completely unplug after church. We would just be together: sitting close, holding hands, cuddling, talking, and making love. We were at each other's attention.

Our family is blended, and it is a beautiful thing to see them now as adults hanging out, laughing, and joking around. Living in unity can be taught. It is a gift that you can pass on to your children. Unity in our home was not negotiable. Some of the rules that supported unity were:

1. Manners to others in and out of the house were required.
2. "Yes, ma'am" or "Yes, sir" was how our kids answered to us.

3. They were not to call one another stepbrothers. They were simply brothers.

4. If any of the brothers argued, they had to serve each other for the day: things like serving them food, pouring them a glass of milk, helping clean their room, etc.…

5. If mom said no, they couldn't go to dad to get a different answer.

6. Never lay your hands on each other.

7. *Never* allow color to be an issue.

8. Eat dinner as a family

When we first married, certain members of Chris's family were not happy that he had married an African-American woman. They ignored our invitation to our wedding. They tried everything to disrupt our unity. They would invite only the light-skinned parts of the family for dinner. When our first son was born, none of them came to see him. Though I knew it must have been tempting to give in to those whom he loved dearly, he never did. My husband would tell them it was all or none because we were a family. If he had given in, it would have opened the door for division between us. I would have questioned his loyalty to me and our uninvited children. Because he protected us, it caused me to draw even closer to him. I knew that he loved me when he was willing to lose his family for us. It was his sacrifice that proved his commitment.

Genesis 2:24 New International Version (NIV) says, "That is why a man leaves his father and mother and is united to his wife, and they become one flesh." Many couples treat marriage as an extension of singleness. Some of the things that you used to do, you can no longer do. It takes work to maintain your marital connection. You can't allow people to come between you; however, there are other things that will try to come between you as well – televisions, the computer, and even work. I am not suggesting that you quit your job or quit watching television, but I am saying that there should be a healthy balance. When we started our business, we always took vacations and it was great. As the business grew, we took fewer and fewer trips. We spent more time working and less time staying connected. This was a clear sign that our balance was off. My husband came home one day and said that he couldn't allow the business to interrupt our connection, so we made some adjustments and scaled back on our workload.

I met with a young lady who shared that her husband didn't like it when she talked to her best friend. He felt that she had a better connection with her than him. I understood what was happening because Chris and I went through this. At the time, I didn't understand what the big deal was when my husband would complain that I told my best friend everything. Although my friend and I had good intentions, it still caused my husband to be resentful. He desired to develop that kind of connection with me, but I had already developed it with her and was a bit protective of it. In order for couples to develop a deeper intimacy, couples must be able to share their deepest thoughts. My best friend and I have been friends for over twenty years, and we still have our connection, but I no longer share more with her than I do my husband. It has been several years since we made this adjustment, and I have no doubt that it was the right thing to do. As a result, it has caused our good marriage to become great. He is my best friend.

Chapter 9:

Money, Why Budget?

Money is the number one reason why people file for divorce. Every couple would agree that money is an important topic, but talking about it is often difficult. When we meet with couples, we ask them what their dreams for their future are. Most would say something like we want to have a nice home and cars, to be able to take yearly vacations, to have a savings account for their future and kid's future. Our next question would be, "What's your business plan to get there?" It is a plan for success. Having a budget in place may seem restrictive, but you are more likely to achieve your goals with one. Setting up a budget should be done as early into the relationship as possible. The good thing is it's never too late to start one.

We met with one young couple to discuss their finances. The

wife complained that her husband liked to spend money as soon as he was paid. She liked to save and was strict with her budget. The husband shared how he worked very hard and should be able to treat himself to whatever he wanted to buy after a hard work week. The wife stated that she wanted to eventually move out of an apartment soon. To their surprise, I told them that a budget would allow for both of them to get their wish. Here are a few of the principles we shared with them.

Write It Down

Discuss what your goals are. Where do you want to be in five, ten, fifteen, or twenty years? Discuss plans for mortgages, vacations, college, savings, retirement, and rainy days. Writing your goals down will serve as a reminder for the both of you when tempted to get off course. If you are both committed to your goals, then the likelihood of you achieving them is very real.

Don't Hide Bank Accounts

This sends a clear message that you are not willing to be in unity in this area. Accounts, once discovered, could carry some heavy consequences. Your spouse may wonder what else is hidden. In any healthy relationship, trust is a must. It doesn't matter who makes the most money or if one partner doesn't make money at all. Couples should make financial decisions together. Just because one partner makes most or all the money doesn't mean that the opinion of your mate should not be valued. For example, if the new car payment will be paid by the husband, that doesn't mean the wife can't express what kind of car she would like.

Who should handle the money?

Years ago, my husband and I discovered that he doesn't like to give attention to money matters. I feel more at ease having a plan in place for avoiding financial stress. I am the budget keeper in our relationship. We review it together, and I listen to his opinion. Your system may be different than ours. The important point is to be sure to have a plan.

Budget and Evaluate

As stated earlier, couples should treat themselves like a business. Evaluate the set budget at least monthly. This meeting should only take up to fifteen to twenty minutes. Determine if the budget needs to be adjusted in any way or if spending should be scaled back. The budget is a small step to ensure that you can attain the larger long-term goal.

Combine, Don't Hide

In marriage, each person should strive for oneness. The decisions about spending money are some of the most important decisions that have to be made, so why not make them together? Some couples have joint accounts for all income. Others have one joint account for reoccurring expenses and then individual accounts for personal spending. I feel that either way works as long as it's agreed upon. Together, decide what amount is reasonable for personal spending to be added to individual accounts. Once it's gone, it's gone.

It will take patience and dedication. You may even experience some frustrations, but if you both commit to a budget, you will find that it deepens your love and respect.

Pray on the Topic Together

Only God knows what our future holds. If you include Him in your financial planning, He will give you wisdom. Have you ever wanted to purchase something you were unsure of? You pray about it, and the next day, you wonder how you ever thought that it was a good idea in the first place. By simply acknowledging God in your finances, it invites Him to direct your paths.

> *"Trust in the Lord with all your heart and do not lean on your own understanding. In all your ways acknowledge Him, and He will make your paths straight."*
> – Proverbs 3:5-6 (NASB)

Tithe

Tithing is a command. When we tithe, we show God that we will be obedient, even in our giving. When we do, God said He will rebuke the devour for us.

> *"Bring all the tithes into the storehouse so there will be enough food in my Temple. If you do," says the Lord of Heaven's Armies, "I will open the windows of heaven for you. I will pour out a blessing so great you won't have enough room to take it in! Try it! Put me to the test! Your crops will be abundant, for I will guard them from insects and disease. Your grapes will not fall from the vine before they are ripe," says the Lord of Heaven's Armies.*
> – Malachi 3:10-11 (NLT)

Chapter 10:

Sex

Whenever we discuss the topic of sex, we usually do so at the end of our lectures intentionally. Great sex isn't something that starts in the bedroom. Great sex is a result of what has happened throughout the days or weeks prior. Remember, sex is not always going to be perfect. Don't compare your sex life with those on TV or at the movies. Create your own special memories through communication, trust, and intimacy. There is no reason why you shouldn't have amazing sex for many years to come.

Staying connected in communication as we stated earlier is key. Talking about the needs of your family or financial matters are important, but talking about the issues of the heart builds intimacy. Unlike most men, it is easy for my husband to be open about his feelings. I was a little more reluctant at first. Sharing my inner thoughts, fantasies, desires, and hurts was a scary place for me. Take baby steps if you are like I was, and test the water. When you find that your mate can be trusted, then share a bit more. I remember telling Chris that I was afraid to share my inner, deepest thoughts. His response was for me to give him a try. You don't want to deny yourself the opportunity to experience this deep love that we have discovered together. Over the years, he has proven that I can trust him. He has never hurt me, no matter how silly or intimate my thoughts have been. He has never laughed or ridiculed me. I now know that I can share anything with him. You might ask, "What does this have to do with sex?" If I can trust him with my crazy thoughts, then I can also trust him with my fantasies. Couples that are willing to share their deepest thoughts, emotions, or fantasies are building trust – protect it!

We met with a couple who was having trouble in the area of sex. The wife complained that she was not satisfied, and the husband was frustrated. I asked the wife if she had shared with her husband what she desired. She stated that he should know if she is enjoying it by her reaction. Don't be afraid to share your sexual desires. Be open and honest without being critical. I discovered years ago that if I focused on learning how to fulfill his needs and he focused on fulfilling mine, we both are fulfilled. It's not your job to fulfill yourself sexually; it's your partner's.

Sexual relations is a process of discovery. Don't fall into the boring trap of doing what you once did to satisfy your partner if it no longer satisfies them. Always look for new ways to keep your fire burning. Try new positions, locations, lingerie. Share what made you feel good and what didn't. Don't make your partner feel like a failure if what they tried didn't fulfill you as it once did. I believe that God created our bodies to constantly change, and sex should be a continuous act of discovery.

> *"Bless your fresh-flowing fountain! Enjoy the wife you married as a young man! Lovely as an angel, beautiful as a rose – don't ever quit taking delight in her body. Never take her love for granted!"*
> – Prov 5:18-19 (MSG)

Sex is a gift to create intimacy and unity. God intended it to be special, fun, and private. Never discuss your sexual encounters with anyone else. This is a guaranteed way to destroy any chances of deeper intimacy. Let your mate know that you desire them by your actions before you get to the bedroom: the way you look at them, your touch, your words.

All throughout the day, my husband reminds me that he desires me in a genuine way. We like to hold hands when walking and even while sitting on the sofa watching a movie. If we hear a song that reminds us of each other, we send a text with the song link. Always exercise the ability to show affection. In the bedroom, there is no doubt that he desires me and I desire him because we have proved it all through the day. This may sound corny, but it has kept our relationship fun and alive for twenty-seven years. No matter how many encounters you have had together, the force of desire can still be there.

Be open to try new things. We met with a couple that had been married around ten years, and they mentioned that they had sex about once a month. It frustrated the wife because she desired it more often. The husband stated that he did too. We were confused and asked what the roadblocks were to prevent more encounters. They looked at each other with a puzzled look. I asked a very simple question that changed their sex life completely. "Do you sleep in pajamas?" They said that they did. My advice to them was to not. Skin to skin creates desire. The following week at the next session, they sat on our couch holding hands and smiling. They said that they were amazed at how something so simple made such a huge impact. They said that they made more love in that week than they ever had in a month.

Make time for each other. In today's society, everyone is busy, but sex is necessary for any marriage to keep it healthy and connected. If you find yourself getting too busy, then schedule a lovemaking date. Some might think that this would be boring;

however, it depends on how you look at it. It can be exciting as you anticipate what's to come. Flirting throughout the day will build anticipation. Just remember that it is a date, so treat it as such. Shave, shower, put your smell-goods on and such. In preparing for the date, you will create sensual anticipation.

The marriage bed is undefiled; however, that doesn't mean that you can do anything in it. Never share your bed with any other sexual partner other than your spouse. Don't introduce anything into sexual relations that make either partner uncomfortable. Be open and willing to discuss your feelings.

Chapter 11:

Obstacles Families May Face

There are many challenges that families face. Statistics show that one in three marriages is a blended family. A blended family indicates that somewhere there is an ex. Dealing with your ex can be challenging. We will discuss how you can keep peace when dealing with them. Another challenge is time or the lack of. Being too busy is a relationship killer. We remember having calendars with something listed on every day. At some point, we had to prioritize.

Time seems to be moving faster, so find the time to continue to grow as a family can be difficult. We are witnesses that blended families can work; however, we are also witnesses that it takes hard work and commitment. Not only are we a blended family, but we are also a bi-racially blended family. We have six sons together. When we first married, we had many conversations between us and our kids. Open dialogue between me and my husband was first and foremost. The kids understood that we would make no decision without each other. Keep in mind that this is something that you have to work at. Many blended families don't survive because parents try putting their kids first as they did prior to marriage. The husband and wife must come first, then the children. Strong families are always built around strong marriages. People resist change, so laying a good foundation of expectation is key.

We had several conversations with our kids together. We would let them know that we loved all of them and that we were now one family. We would describe our marriage to the kids as us being best friends and that best friends must stick together. They seemed to understand this concept when they were young. It is important that they respect your union.

When step-parenting, patience is also key. It is difficult enough to become one with your new mate. Adding step kids in the mix is even more challenging. I was a single mom of one child, a three-year-old son. Within one year, I ended up with my son, two stepsons, and another son between us who was born in our first year of marriage. They were all so different, and it was their differences that drove me bananas. They all had different needs, sleep habits, eating habits, developmental differences, just to name a few. My husband's oldest son was used to sleeping with his father. I was not used to that and was never willing to share my bed with anyone except for my husband. He would cry and beg to stay with his father, but we never gave in. To help him process this change emotionally, my husband would read to him before bed and would lay next to him until he fell asleep. Within a few months, he was falling asleep on his own. I would remind myself that it would get better and to just be patient, and it did.

When blending two families, we worked hard to let them know that we would act fairly and equally to the best of our ability. Parents that don't fully adopt the same standards for the children open the door for resentment toward each other. In all of our twenty-seven years of marriage, we have never heard any of the boys say that we treated any of them more favorably than another. I remember when the grandmother of my husband's sons came into town. She gave one of them sixty dollars and nothing to the rest of the boys. As soon as we got into our van, I reached my hand back and requested the money. He replied that it was his money that his grandmother had given it to him. I reminded him that we needed to continue to grow in unity as a family. I took the money, and we all went out to eat and bowling together. This was our way of demonstrating that we are going to be a united family and that they would all be treated the same.

Planning fun activities with the kids was a weekly occurrence. We noticed that the boys seemed to grow closer when they were having fun. We would take them camping, fishing, and swimming. It was enjoyable to hear them laughing together. They were building friendships. With so many new changes in their lives as we merge together, it was important to make it as fun as possible.

Building relationships and trust within the family calls for your presence. All the boys loved sports, which was a great outlet for releasing pent-up energy. They played football, baseball, wrestling, and basketball. My husband and I were present for all their events. I was team mom for most of their teams, and my husband coached. I was also a stepchild to a wonderful stepmom. I had a small role in our school play. The play lasted for six hours – three hours for two consecutive nights. She came and sat in the audience both nights. I still remember it, and it was over thirty-five years ago. Giving your time says you care.

Never show the kids that you don't agree with each other. Kids are generally selfish. They want what they want, and if they see that mom and dad are not unified, they will use it to their advantage. Always discuss disagreements privately. Resist the temptation of allowing them to come between you, even if you agree with the kids. We would even ask the kids to be patient before we would answer their questions. We first wanted to ensure we were both on the same page. Whatever our decision was, we would explain it with the kids together. If unable to resolve any conflict, seek counseling. Sometimes you may need an unbiased listener.

Now, about the ex-wife/husband: Keeping peace with them is not only good for the kids but also for you. This will always be tricky no matter how hard you try. Here are a few tips to remind couples:

- Decide on the best way to communicate. Technology has provided the easiest way to communicate, but don't allow it to become your weapon of choice. Stick to the facts; don't criticize or attack.
- Don't be in a hurry to respond back, and proofread your response before you push send.
- Acknowledge that you heard your ex's opinions/concerns.
- Even when they are ridiculous! This level of respect will defuse them.
- Stick to the court order. This is in place to help avoid entering the gray areas with them. If they want to argue about what's in the court order, then they can take that up with the courts.
- Keep the kids out of the middle. They are already upset that their parents can't get along.

Chapter 12:

Get Ready to Start a Movement

We believe a desire to bring hope and change to marriages is your calling. Couples are struggling while divorce rates are climbing. The cycle continues from one generation to the next. Sharing the principles in my book with your clients will cause many to work through conflicts and crisis. With the information presented, you have the opportunity to change the course of many lives, just as my husband and I have. The fire of passion for marriages should be more ignited. Feel confident that the contents of this book aren't just knowledge but rather personal experiences that worked.

When we started helping couples, we had no idea what to say, so we shared simple truths through our desire to bring change. As we shared from the heart, God would begin to direct our words. The key is to simply start. We had never gone to a bible college to learn what we share, yet couples still seek us out. They will know if you have a genuine concern for them; they can feel it. Many of the couples that we have worked with had already gone through counseling elsewhere. They would say that it was life-changing because it was presented in a way that is understandable. Just as our classes kept growing because of faithfulness, yours will too.

When teaching marriage conferences or one-on-ones, we teach the same principles in this book. They are foundational and should be applied in all marriages. We have found that some marriages have never applied many of the principles and others just need a tune-up. Adapting the techniques and teachings written in this book will help you develop your own process that will help couples become better versions of themselves.

After reading this book, you should be well equipped to teach a marriage class. The subjects are separated in a way that you would be able to teach from topics. You should be able to provide them with key scriptures that apply. You should be able to demonstrate sharing the personal stories to the principle. We have formulated this easy-to-read tool in such a way that even a beginner would be able to teach a marriage class. If you feel the call stronger now than ever, then it's time to make a difference. Don't miss your call.

Acknowledgments

Pastor Angie

I want to dedicate this book to Mrs. Regina Smith for being the vessel that God used to speak life into what I only dreamed possible. Thank you, my little angel! I would like to sincerely thank my husband who has been my rock! He has fought for us. He has never grown tired of showing his love. He has taught me what real love is. Without his commitment to God, our children, and me, there would be no book. I want to deeply thank God for sending my husband and for choosing me to be his handmaiden in helping restore His institution of marriage. What an honor. A special thanks to our six sons for sticking with us through the merging of our families and for loving each other through the process. I would also like to thank

Pastor Doneta Warren for speaking into my life. It was because of her prophetic word that I was brave enough to step out on faith and trust God through a tough season.

Pastor Chris

I first must thank God for being patient with me while his plans for my life unfolded. I would like to thank my Mom and Dad for being a good example of what a marriage should look like. A special thanks goes to Bill and Jeanie Burton who took my sons and me in at a very low point. Without their Godly wisdom, I wouldn't have been equipped for this season in life. I wish to thank my wife for always believing in me. You never quit loving and trusting in me. I can truly say that you have become my best friend and lover.

Thank you to Angela Lauria and The Author Incubator's team, as well as to David Hancock and the Morgan James Publishing team for helping me bring this book to print.

Thank You

Thank you for taking to time read our book! We desire that you be successful in the mission of restoring families. If you would like to reach us, you can do so easily on our Facebook page entitled: Unified Family Coaching.

https://www.facebook.com/REAL-Marriage-with-the-Youseys-103035677727274/

or

www.coachyousey.com

About the Authors

Angela Yousey and her husband Chris co-pastor at the Spirit of Love Ministries in Columbus, Ohio. For nearly twenty-seven years, they have worked with couples and families providing them with sound biblical counseling. They first started with small groups in their home, per the request of a few struggling couples. The groups grew so large that people would sit on the floor. Because of their dedication and ability to deliver a message of hope, their following evolved into a church that launched in 2018. Angela loves helping people. Her career choice was a registered nurse. She has practiced in her career for twenty-eight years.

Angela and her husband had both been divorced when they met. They understand what it takes to overcome the emotional pain of divorce after living through it. She felt that all of her struggles and pain was part of God's plan. She says that even as a child she knew she would one day help marriages. When she met her husband, he also desired to help restore marriages. They have been able to blend their two families together into a loving one. Together they have six sons and six grandchildren. Four of their sons served in the United States Armed Forces, and one earned a full football scholarship to the University of Toledo. Their last son is currently being recruited by several Division I colleges for football. Her story is a demonstration of the power of love, unity, and grace.

9 781642 797206